THIS

Meeting Agenda Notebook

BELONGS TO:

DEDICATION

This Meeting Notes Journal is dedicated to all the people out there who take meeting notes and document their findings in the process.

You are my inspiration for producing books and I'm honored to be a part of keeping all of your Meeting notes, and records organized.

This journal notebook will help you record your details about your meetings.

Thoughtfully put together with these sections to record: Purpose, Venue, Date & Time, Note Taker, Facilitator, Attendees, Agenda, Deliverable & Notes.

HOW TO USE THIS BOOK

The purpose of this book is to keep all of your Meeting notes all in one place. It will help keep you organized.

This Meeting Notes Journal will allow you to accurately document every detail about your meetings. It's a great way to chart your course by taking accurate notes.

Here are examples of the prompts for you to fill in and write about your experience in this book:

1. Purpose - Write the purpose of the meeting.

2. Venue - Log where the meeting was held.

3. Date & Time - Record the date and time of the meeting.

4. Note Taker - Write who was taking notes for the meeting.

5. Facilitator - Log the name of the facilitator.

6. Attendees - Record everyone present at the meeting.

7. Agenda Item & Presenter - Write the agenda item & who the presenter was.

8. Deliverable - Log who is to carry out the action and date completed.

9. Notes - Record any other additional important information.

Purpose _____

Venue _____ Date & Time _____

Note Taker _____ Facilitator _____

Attendees	
Name	Contact Information

Agenda Item	Presenter

Deliverable	Initials	Completed

Notes

Purpose _____

Venue _____ Date & Time _____

Note Taker _____ Facilitator _____

Attendees	
Name	Contact Information

Agenda Item	Presenter

Deliverable	Initials	Completed

Notes

Purpose _____

Venue _____ Date & Time _____

Note Taker _____ Facilitator _____

Attendees	
Name	Contact Information

Agenda Item	Presenter	Deliverable	Initials	Completed

Notes

Purpose _____

Venue _____ Date & Time _____

Note Taker _____ Facilitator _____

Attendees	
Name	Contact Information

Agenda Item	Presenter		Deliverable	Initials	Completed

Notes

Purpose _____

Venue _____ Date & Time _____

Note Taker _____ Facilitator _____

Attendees	
Name	Contact Information

Agenda Item	Presenter		Deliverable	Initials	Completed

Notes

Purpose _____

Venue _____ Date & Time _____

Note Taker _____ Facilitator _____

Attendees	
Name	Contact Information

Agenda Item	Presenter		Deliverable	Initials	Completed

Notes

Purpose _____

Venue _____ Date & Time _____

Note Taker _____ Facilitator _____

Attendees	
Name	Contact Information

Agenda Item	Presenter		Deliverable	Initials	Completed

Notes

Purpose _____

Venue _____   Date & Time _____

Note Taker _____   Facilitator _____

Attendees	
Name	Contact Information

Agenda Item	Presenter	Deliverable	Initials	Completed

Notes

Purpose _____

Venue _____ Date & Time _____

Note Taker _____ Facilitator _____

Attendees	
Name	Contact Information

Agenda Item	Presenter	Deliverable	Initials	Completed

Notes

Purpose _____

Venue _____ Date & Time _____

Note Taker _____ Facilitator _____

Attendees	
Name	Contact Information

Agenda Item	Presenter

Deliverable	Initials	Completed

Notes

Purpose _____

Venue _____ Date & Time _____

Note Taker _____ Facilitator _____

Attendees	
Name	Contact Information

Agenda Item	Presenter	Deliverable	Initials	Completed

Notes

Purpose _____

Venue _____ Date & Time _____

Note Taker _____ Facilitator _____

Attendees	
Name	Contact Information

Agenda Item	Presenter		Deliverable	Initials	Completed

Notes

Purpose _____

Venue _____ Date & Time _____

Note Taker _____ Facilitator _____

Attendees	
Name	Contact Information

Agenda Item	Presenter	Deliverable	Initials	Completed

Notes

Purpose _____

Venue _____ Date & Time _____

Note Taker _____ Facilitator _____

Attendees	
Name	Contact Information

Agenda Item	Presenter

Deliverable	Initials	Completed

Notes

Purpose _____

Venue _____ Date & Time _____

Note Taker _____ Facilitator _____

Attendees	
Name	Contact Information

Agenda Item	Presenter

Deliverable	Initials	Completed

Notes

Purpose _____

Venue _____ Date & Time _____

Note Taker _____ Facilitator _____

Attendees	
Name	Contact Information

Agenda Item	Presenter		Deliverable	Initials	Completed

Notes

Purpose _____

Venue _____ Date & Time _____

Note Taker _____ Facilitator _____

Attendees	
Name	Contact Information

Agenda Item	Presenter

Deliverable	Initials	Completed

Notes

Purpose _____

Venue _____   Date & Time _____

Note Taker _____   Facilitator _____

Attendees	
Name	Contact Information

Agenda Item	Presenter	Deliverable	Initials	Completed

Notes

Purpose _____

Venue _____   Date & Time _____

Note Taker _____   Facilitator _____

Attendees	
Name	Contact Information

Agenda Item	Presenter

Deliverable	Initials	Completed

Notes

Purpose _____

Venue _____ Date & Time _____

Note Taker _____ Facilitator _____

Attendees	
Name	Contact Information

Agenda Item	Presenter	Deliverable	Initials	Completed

Notes

Purpose _____

Venue _____ Date & Time _____

Note Taker _____ Facilitator _____

Attendees	
Name	Contact Information

Agenda Item	Presenter	Deliverable	Initials	Completed

Notes

Purpose _____

Venue _____ Date & Time _____

Note Taker _____ Facilitator _____

Attendees	
Name	Contact Information

Agenda Item	Presenter		Deliverable	Initials	Completed

Notes

Purpose _____

Venue _____ Date & Time _____

Note Taker _____ Facilitator _____

Attendees	
Name	Contact Information

Agenda Item	Presenter		Deliverable	Initials	Completed

Notes

Purpose _____

Venue _____ Date & Time _____

Note Taker _____ Facilitator _____

Attendees	
Name	Contact Information

Agenda Item	Presenter		Deliverable	Initials	Completed

Notes

Purpose _____

Venue _____ Date & Time _____

Note Taker _____ Facilitator _____

Attendees	
Name	Contact Information

Agenda Item	Presenter		Deliverable	Initials	Completed

Notes

Purpose _____

Venue _____ Date & Time _____

Note Taker _____ Facilitator _____

Attendees	
Name	Contact Information

Agenda Item	Presenter	Deliverable	Initials	Completed

Notes

Purpose _____

Venue _____   Date & Time _____

Note Taker _____   Facilitator _____

Attendees	
Name	Contact Information

Agenda Item	Presenter		Deliverable	Initials	Completed

Notes

Purpose _____

Venue _____ Date & Time _____

Note Taker _____ Facilitator _____

Attendees	
Name	Contact Information

Agenda Item	Presenter		Deliverable	Initials	Completed

Notes

Purpose _____

Venue _____ Date & Time _____

Note Taker _____ Facilitator _____

Attendees	
Name	Contact Information

Agenda Item	Presenter		Deliverable	Initials	Completed

Notes

Purpose   _____

Venue   _____   Date & Time   _____

Note Taker   _____   Facilitator   _____

Attendees	
Name	Contact Information

Agenda Item	Presenter

Deliverable	Initials	Completed

Notes

Purpose _____

Venue _____ Date & Time _____

Note Taker _____ Facilitator _____

Attendees	
Name	Contact Information

Agenda Item	Presenter	Deliverable	Initials	Completed

Notes

Purpose _____

Venue _____ Date & Time _____

Note Taker _____ Facilitator _____

Attendees	
Name	Contact Information

Agenda Item	Presenter

Deliverable	Initials	Completed

Notes

Purpose _____

Venue _____   Date & Time _____

Note Taker _____   Facilitator _____

Attendees	
Name	Contact Information

Agenda Item	Presenter

Deliverable	Initials	Completed

Notes

Purpose _____

Venue _____ Date & Time _____

Note Taker _____ Facilitator _____

Attendees	
Name	Contact Information

Agenda Item	Presenter		Deliverable	Initials	Completed

Notes

Purpose _____

Venue _____   Date & Time _____

Note Taker _____   Facilitator _____

Attendees	
Name	Contact Information

Agenda Item	Presenter		Deliverable	Initials	Completed

Notes

Purpose _____

Venue _____ Date & Time _____

Note Taker _____ Facilitator _____

Attendees	
Name	Contact Information

Agenda Item	Presenter		Deliverable	Initials	Completed

Notes

Purpose _____

Venue _____ Date & Time _____

Note Taker _____ Facilitator _____

Attendees	
Name	Contact Information

Agenda Item	Presenter	Deliverable	Initials	Completed

Notes

Purpose _____

Venue _____ Date & Time _____

Note Taker _____ Facilitator _____

Attendees	
Name	Contact Information

Agenda Item	Presenter		Deliverable	Initials	Completed

Notes

Purpose _____

Venue _____ Date & Time _____

Note Taker _____ Facilitator _____

Attendees	
Name	Contact Information

Agenda Item	Presenter		Deliverable	Initials	Completed

Notes

Purpose _____

Venue _____ Date & Time _____

Note Taker _____ Facilitator _____

Attendees	
Name	Contact Information

Agenda Item	Presenter

Deliverable	Initials	Completed

Notes

Purpose _____

Venue _____ Date & Time _____

Note Taker _____ Facilitator _____

Attendees	
Name	Contact Information

Agenda Item	Presenter		Deliverable	Initials	Completed

Notes

Purpose _____

Venue _____ Date & Time _____

Note Taker _____ Facilitator _____

Attendees	
Name	Contact Information

Agenda Item	Presenter		Deliverable	Initials	Completed

Notes

Purpose _____

Venue _____   Date & Time _____

Note Taker _____   Facilitator _____

Attendees	
Name	Contact Information

Agenda Item	Presenter

Deliverable	Initials	Completed

Notes

Purpose _____

Venue _____ Date & Time _____

Note Taker _____ Facilitator _____

Attendees	
Name	Contact Information

Agenda Item	Presenter		Deliverable	Initials	Completed

Notes

_____

Purpose _____

Venue _____ Date & Time _____

Note Taker _____ Facilitator _____

Attendees	
Name	Contact Information

Agenda Item	Presenter

Deliverable	Initials	Completed

Notes

Purpose _____

Venue _____ Date & Time _____

Note Taker _____ Facilitator _____

Attendees	
Name	Contact Information

Agenda Item	Presenter	Deliverable	Initials	Completed

Notes

Purpose _____

Venue _____ Date & Time _____

Note Taker _____ Facilitator _____

Attendees	
Name	Contact Information

Agenda Item	Presenter	Deliverable	Initials	Completed

Notes

Purpose _____

Venue _____ Date & Time _____

Note Taker _____ Facilitator _____

Attendees	
Name	Contact Information

Agenda Item	Presenter		Deliverable	Initials	Completed

Notes

Purpose _____

Venue _____ Date & Time _____

Note Taker _____ Facilitator _____

Attendees	
Name	Contact Information

Agenda Item	Presenter		Deliverable	Initials	Completed

Notes

Purpose _____

Venue _____ Date & Time _____

Note Taker _____ Facilitator _____

Attendees	
Name	Contact Information

Agenda Item	Presenter		Deliverable	Initials	Completed

Notes

Purpose _____

Venue _____   Date & Time _____

Note Taker _____   Facilitator _____

Attendees	
Name	Contact Information

Agenda Item	Presenter	Deliverable	Initials	Completed

Notes

Purpose _____

Venue _____ Date & Time _____

Note Taker _____ Facilitator _____

Attendees	
Name	Contact Information

Agenda Item	Presenter		Deliverable	Initials	Completed

Notes

Purpose _____

Venue _____   Date & Time _____

Note Taker _____   Facilitator _____

Attendees	
Name	Contact Information

Agenda Item	Presenter	Deliverable	Initials	Completed

Notes

Purpose _____

Venue _____ Date & Time _____

Note Taker _____ Facilitator _____

Attendees	
Name	Contact Information

Agenda Item	Presenter

Deliverable	Initials	Completed

Notes

Purpose _____

Venue _____ Date & Time _____

Note Taker _____ Facilitator _____

Attendees	
Name	Contact Information

Agenda Item	Presenter	Deliverable	Initials	Completed

Notes

Purpose _____

Venue _____ Date & Time _____

Note Taker _____ Facilitator _____

Attendees	
Name	Contact Information

Agenda Item	Presenter		Deliverable	Initials	Completed

Notes

Purpose _____

Venue _____ Date & Time _____

Note Taker _____ Facilitator _____

Attendees	
Name	Contact Information

Agenda Item	Presenter		Deliverable	Initials	Completed

Notes

Purpose _____

Venue _____   Date & Time _____

Note Taker _____   Facilitator _____

Attendees	
Name	Contact Information

Agenda Item	Presenter

Deliverable	Initials	Completed

Notes

_____

Purpose _____

Venue _____ Date & Time _____

Note Taker _____ Facilitator _____

Attendees	
Name	Contact Information

Agenda Item	Presenter

Deliverable	Initials	Completed

Notes

Purpose _____

Venue _____ Date & Time _____

Note Taker _____ Facilitator _____

Attendees	
Name	Contact Information

Agenda Item	Presenter		Deliverable	Initials	Completed

Notes

Purpose _____

Venue _____ Date & Time _____

Note Taker _____ Facilitator _____

Attendees	
Name	Contact Information

Agenda Item	Presenter

Deliverable	Initials	Completed

Notes

Purpose _____

Venue _____   Date & Time _____

Note Taker _____   Facilitator _____

Attendees	
Name	Contact Information

Agenda Item	Presenter		Deliverable	Initials	Completed

Notes

Purpose _____

Venue _____ Date & Time _____

Note Taker _____ Facilitator _____

Attendees	
Name	Contact Information

Agenda Item	Presenter

Deliverable	Initials	Completed

Notes

Purpose _____

Venue _____ Date & Time _____

Note Taker _____ Facilitator _____

Attendees	
Name	Contact Information

Agenda Item	Presenter

Deliverable	Initials	Completed

Notes

_____

Purpose _____

Venue _____ Date & Time _____

Note Taker _____ Facilitator _____

Attendees	
Name	Contact Information

Agenda Item	Presenter		Deliverable	Initials	Completed

Notes

Purpose _____

Venue _____ Date & Time _____

Note Taker _____ Facilitator _____

Attendees	
Name	Contact Information

Agenda Item	Presenter

Deliverable	Initials	Completed

Notes

Purpose _____

Venue _____ Date & Time _____

Note Taker _____ Facilitator _____

Attendees	
Name	Contact Information

Agenda Item	Presenter

Deliverable	Initials	Completed

Notes

Purpose _____

Venue _____ Date & Time _____

Note Taker _____ Facilitator _____

Attendees	
Name	Contact Information

Agenda Item	Presenter

Deliverable	Initials	Completed

Notes

Purpose _____

Venue _____ Date & Time _____

Note Taker _____ Facilitator _____

Attendees	
Name	Contact Information

Agenda Item	Presenter		Deliverable	Initials	Completed

Notes

Purpose _____

Venue _____ Date & Time _____

Note Taker _____ Facilitator _____

Attendees	
Name	Contact Information

Agenda Item	Presenter	Deliverable	Initials	Completed

Notes

Purpose _____

Venue _____   Date & Time _____

Note Taker _____   Facilitator _____

Attendees	
Name	Contact Information

Agenda Item	Presenter

Deliverable	Initials	Completed

Notes

Purpose _____

Venue _____ Date & Time _____

Note Taker _____ Facilitator _____

Attendees	
Name	Contact Information

Agenda Item	Presenter	Deliverable	Initials	Completed

Notes

Purpose _____

Venue _____ Date & Time _____

Note Taker _____ Facilitator _____

Attendees	
Name	Contact Information

Agenda Item	Presenter	Deliverable	Initials	Completed

Notes

Purpose _____

Venue _____ Date & Time _____

Note Taker _____ Facilitator _____

Attendees	
Name	Contact Information

Agenda Item	Presenter

Deliverable	Initials	Completed

Notes

_____

Purpose _____

Venue _____   Date & Time _____

Note Taker _____   Facilitator _____

Attendees	
Name	Contact Information

Agenda Item	Presenter

Deliverable	Initials	Completed

Notes

Purpose _____

Venue _____ Date & Time _____

Note Taker _____ Facilitator _____

Attendees	
Name	Contact Information

Agenda Item	Presenter		Deliverable	Initials	Completed

Notes

Purpose _____

Venue _____ Date & Time _____

Note Taker _____ Facilitator _____

Attendees	
Name	Contact Information

Agenda Item	Presenter	Deliverable	Initials	Completed

Notes

Purpose _____

Venue _____ Date & Time _____

Note Taker _____ Facilitator _____

Attendees	
Name	Contact Information

Agenda Item	Presenter

Deliverable	Initials	Completed

Notes

Purpose _____

Venue _____   Date & Time _____

Note Taker _____   Facilitator _____

Attendees	
Name	Contact Information

Agenda Item	Presenter		Deliverable	Initials	Completed

Notes

Purpose _____

Venue _____ Date & Time _____

Note Taker _____ Facilitator _____

Attendees	
Name	Contact Information

Agenda Item	Presenter	Deliverable	Initials	Completed

Notes

Purpose _____

Venue _____ Date & Time _____

Note Taker _____ Facilitator _____

Attendees	
Name	Contact Information

Agenda Item	Presenter		Deliverable	Initials	Completed

Notes

Purpose _____

Venue _____ Date & Time _____

Note Taker _____ Facilitator _____

Attendees	
Name	Contact Information

Agenda Item	Presenter		Deliverable	Initials	Completed

Notes

Purpose _____

Venue _____ Date & Time _____

Note Taker _____ Facilitator _____

Attendees	
Name	Contact Information

Agenda Item	Presenter

Deliverable	Initials	Completed

Notes

Purpose _____

Venue _____ Date & Time _____

Note Taker _____ Facilitator _____

Attendees

Name	Contact Information

Agenda Item	Presenter		Deliverable	Initials	Completed

Notes

Purpose _____

Venue _____ Date & Time _____

Note Taker _____ Facilitator _____

Attendees	
Name	Contact Information

Agenda Item	Presenter	Deliverable	Initials	Completed

Notes

_____

Purpose _____

Venue _____ Date & Time _____

Note Taker _____ Facilitator _____

Attendees	
Name	Contact Information

Agenda Item	Presenter

Deliverable	Initials	Completed

Notes

Purpose _____

Venue _____ Date & Time _____

Note Taker _____ Facilitator _____

Attendees	
Name	Contact Information

Agenda Item	Presenter

Deliverable	Initials	Completed

Notes

Purpose _____

Venue _____ Date & Time _____

Note Taker _____ Facilitator _____

Attendees	
Name	Contact Information

Agenda Item	Presenter		Deliverable	Initials	Completed

Notes

Purpose _____

Venue _____ Date & Time _____

Note Taker _____ Facilitator _____

Attendees	
Name	Contact Information

Agenda Item	Presenter

Deliverable	Initials	Completed

Notes

Purpose _____

Venue _____   Date & Time _____

Note Taker _____   Facilitator _____

Attendees	
Name	Contact Information

Agenda Item	Presenter	Deliverable	Initials	Completed

Notes

_____

Purpose _____

Venue _____ Date & Time _____

Note Taker _____ Facilitator _____

Attendees	
Name	Contact Information

Agenda Item	Presenter		Deliverable	Initials	Completed

Notes

Purpose _____

Venue _____ Date & Time _____

Note Taker _____ Facilitator _____

Attendees	
Name	Contact Information

Agenda Item	Presenter

Deliverable	Initials	Completed

Notes

_____

Purpose _____

Venue _____ Date & Time _____

Note Taker _____ Facilitator _____

Attendees	
Name	Contact Information

Agenda Item	Presenter

Deliverable	Initials	Completed

Notes

Purpose _____

Venue _____ Date & Time _____

Note Taker _____ Facilitator _____

Attendees	
Name	Contact Information

Agenda Item	Presenter

Deliverable	Initials	Completed

Notes

Purpose _____

Venue _____ Date & Time _____

Note Taker _____ Facilitator _____

Attendees	
Name	Contact Information

Agenda Item	Presenter		Deliverable	Initials	Completed

Notes

Purpose _____

Venue _____   Date & Time _____

Note Taker _____   Facilitator _____

Attendees	
Name	Contact Information

Agenda Item	Presenter

Deliverable	Initials	Completed

Notes

```



```

Purpose _____

Venue _____ Date & Time _____

Note Taker _____ Facilitator _____

Attendees	
Name	Contact Information

Agenda Item	Presenter

Deliverable	Initials	Completed

Notes

Purpose _____

Venue _____   Date & Time _____

Note Taker _____   Facilitator _____

Attendees	
Name	Contact Information

Agenda Item	Presenter	Deliverable	Initials	Completed

Notes

Purpose _____

Venue _____   Date & Time _____

Note Taker _____   Facilitator _____

Attendees	
Name	Contact Information

Agenda Item	Presenter

Deliverable	Initials	Completed

Notes

Purpose _____

Venue _____ Date & Time _____

Note Taker _____ Facilitator _____

Attendees	
Name	Contact Information

Agenda Item	Presenter		Deliverable	Initials	Completed

Notes

_____

Purpose _____

Venue _____ Date & Time _____

Note Taker _____ Facilitator _____

Attendees	
Name	Contact Information

Agenda Item	Presenter

Deliverable	Initials	Completed

Notes

Purpose _____

Venue _____   Date & Time _____

Note Taker _____   Facilitator _____

Attendees	
Name	Contact Information

Agenda Item	Presenter

Deliverable	Initials	Completed

Notes

Purpose _____

Venue _____   Date & Time _____

Note Taker _____   Facilitator _____

Attendees	
Name	Contact Information

Agenda Item	Presenter		Deliverable	Initials	Completed

Notes

Purpose _____

Venue _____ Date & Time _____

Note Taker _____ Facilitator _____

Attendees	
Name	Contact Information

Agenda Item	Presenter		Deliverable	Initials	Completed

Notes

Purpose _____

Venue _____ Date & Time _____

Note Taker _____ Facilitator _____

Attendees	
Name	Contact Information

Agenda Item	Presenter

Deliverable	Initials	Completed

Notes

Purpose _____

Venue _____ Date & Time _____

Note Taker _____ Facilitator _____

Attendees	
Name	Contact Information

Agenda Item	Presenter		Deliverable	Initials	Completed

Notes

Purpose _____

Venue _____ Date & Time _____

Note Taker _____ Facilitator _____

Attendees	
Name	Contact Information

Agenda Item	Presenter

Deliverable	Initials	Completed

Notes

Purpose _____

Venue _____ Date & Time _____

Note Taker _____ Facilitator _____

Attendees	
Name	Contact Information

Agenda Item	Presenter		Deliverable	Initials	Completed

Notes

Purpose _____

Venue _____   Date & Time _____

Note Taker _____   Facilitator _____

Attendees	
Name	Contact Information

Agenda Item	Presenter

Deliverable	Initials	Completed

Notes